MACHIAVELLI UNVEILED

Unearthing the Depths of Power, Morality, and Political Interpretations

Alfonso Borello

Villaggio Publishing Ltd

CONTENTS

PREFACE

In the realm of political philosophy, few figures have left as indelible a mark as Niccolò Machiavelli. His works, most notably "The Prince," have sparked centuries of intellectual discourse and debate, captivating the minds of scholars, thinkers, and leaders alike. Machiavelli's ideas continue to resonate, challenging conventional notions of power, morality, and the complexities of political life.

This book is an exploration into the intricate layers of interpretation that surround Machiavelli's ideas. It delves deep into the rich tapestry of his writings, seeking to uncover the multifaceted meanings embedded within his texts. It is an invitation to navigate the labyrinth of Machiavelli's thought, examining the intersections of realism and idealism, amorality and morality, power and ethics.

Each chapter of this book peels back a different layer, exposing the diverse lenses through which Machiavelli's works have been viewed throughout history. We embark on a journey that transcends time, exploring the historical context that shaped Machiavelli's thinking and the turbulent political landscape of Renaissance Italy, which provided the backdrop for his writings.

The interpretations we encounter along the way range from those who see Machiavelli as a pragmatic realist, providing shrewd guidance for navigating the treacherous waters of politics, to those who discern a deeper moral and ethical dimension to his ideas, where the pursuit of power intersects with questions of virtue and responsibility.

Moreover, we delve into the enduring influence of Machiavelli's works. We examine how his ideas have shaped subsequent political thought, from the realms of political theory to the corridors of power, influencing both thinkers and leaders in their understanding of the complexities of governance.

This work serves as a guide, shedding light on the various layers of interpretation that have emerged over time, offering readers a nuanced understanding of Machiavelli's intellectual legacy. It encourages critical engagement with his ideas, recognizing the importance of grappling with the timeless questions he posed about power, morality, and the inherent dilemmas of political leadership.

As we embark on this intellectual journey through the prism of Machiavelli's thought, let us approach his ideas with an open mind, ready to explore the intricacies of his philosophy and uncover the hidden depths that lie within. Together, let us unravel the enigmatic tapestry of Machiavelli's political discourse and gain fresh insights into the complexities of the human condition in the pursuit and exercise of power.

May this exploration ignite new discussions, inspire further scholarship, and shed light on the enduring relevance of Machiavelli's ideas in our ever-evolving political landscape.

A RISING PHOENIX: THE INTELLECTUAL JOURNEY OF NICCOLÒ MACHIAVELLI IN THE TUSCAN SUN

In the picturesque village of San Casciano, nestled amidst rolling hills and basking in the golden Tuscan sun, a legend was born on a radiant May morning. The date was the third of May in the year 1469 when Niccolò Machiavelli graced the world with his presence. Born into a lineage of nobility, his father, the esteemed Bernardo Machiavelli, was renowned for his astute legal prowess, while his mother, the enchanting Bartolomea Di Stefano Nelli, possessed a lineage steeped in wealth and opulence, derived from her merchant heritage.

Though Bernardo possessed an astute legal mind, his entrepreneurial ventures and ill-fated financial decisions led him down a treacherous path. Plagued by mounting debts, he found himself ensnared in a web of financial burdens that eventually led to his defaulting on loans. This unfortunate turn of events cast a pall of disrepute upon his family's name, rendering him ineligible for public office, which demanded unwavering financial integrity.

Within the quaint embrace of their small villa, Bernardo carried out his legal practice in clandestine fashion. Hidden away from prying eyes, this humble abode served as a sanctuary for both father and son, providing a haven where young Niccolò could embark on his intellectual odyssey.

The Machiavelli villa held a treasure trove of knowledge within its walls. A modest library, its shelves adorned with weathered tomes, became the sanctuary where Niccolò's voracious appetite for learning found sustenance. Here, surrounded by the scent of aging parchment and the hushed whispers of ancient wisdom, he whiled away countless hours, engrossed in the profound thoughts of scholars who had come before him.

In this hallowed space, Niccolò immersed himself in the intoxicating embrace of languages. The eloquent melodies of Latin and the captivating nuances of Greek unfurled before his eager gaze. Guided by the words of classical thinkers and poets, he ventured into realms of thought that expanded his horizons, unveiling the intricacies of human expression and the profound ideas that lay hidden within ancient texts.

Yet, the specifics of Machiavelli's formal education remain elusive, shrouded in the mists of time. While his studies in Latin and Greek are widely acknowledged, the precise details of his academic journey remain enigmatic. It is as if the young prodigy defied the confines of traditional educational systems, blazing his own trail through the realms of knowledge, guided by his insatiable curiosity and an unquenchable thirst for understanding.

Inside the walls of the small villa, Niccolò Machiavelli emerged as a self-made scholar, a polymath who gleaned knowledge from the books that lined his father's shelves. The absence of formal education only served to enhance his reputation, as it became evident that his intellectual prowess transcended the boundaries of institutional learning. It was through his innate thirst for knowledge and his relentless pursuit of enlightenment that the man who said "the ends justify the means" emerged as a formidable thinker, poised to make an indelible mark on the world stage.

Amidst this tempestuous backdrop, Niccolò Machiavelli emerged as a beacon of resilience and intellectual prowess. He weathered the storms of his family's financial downfall with remarkable grace, transforming adversity into an opportunity for personal growth and introspection. The constraints imposed by his father's tarnished reputation only fueled his determination to carve his own path, unburdened by the mistakes of the past.

Driven by an insatiable thirst for knowledge, Machiavelli delved deep into the annals of history, seeking solace and wisdom in the lives and writings of great thinkers and leaders who had faced their own trials and tribulations. He understood that adversity was not a barrier, but rather a crucible that shaped character and fueled innovation.

THE RENAISSANCE CRUCIBLE: MACHIAVELLI'S FORMATIVE YEARS IN THE RADIANT CITY OF FLORENCE

In the luminous dawn of Niccolò Machiavelli's birth, Florence stood as a thriving city-state, its destiny intertwined with the illustrious reign of Lorenzo De Medici. The Medici family, with their astute patronage and far-reaching influence, had elevated Florence to unprecedented heights of prosperity and cultural brilliance. Within the confines of its walls, Florence pulsated with a vibrant energy, an embodiment of a self-governed entity that defied the oppressive chains of the Signorie, the territories ruled by solitary men.

While the Signorie exerted their dominion with an iron grip, stifling the voices of the populace and monopolizing power, Florence flourished under the nurturing hands of Lorenzo De Medici. His enlightened rule breathed life into the city's democratic spirit, fostering an environment where the arts, sciences, and commerce could thrive harmoniously. Florence became a beacon of intellectual enlightenment and progressive thinking, attracting luminaries from all corners of the known world.

Lorenzo De Medici's enlightened governance nurtured a fertile ground for Machiavelli's formative years. As the young prodigy observed the workings of the city-state, he imbibed the essence of democratic ideals, witnessing firsthand the triumphs of a self-ruled society. This profound experience instilled within him an unwavering belief in the power of collective governance, the potential for a people united under a shared vision to achieve greatness.

Amidst the flourishing splendor of Florence, Machiavelli honed his intellect, engaging in lively debates and forging deep connections with fellow intellectuals who congregated in the city's bustling squares. It was in this milieu of intellectual ferment that Machiavelli's mind expanded, assimilating diverse perspectives and refining his own philosophical outlook.

As he grew, the young author of 'The Prince' became acutely aware of the contrasting fate of other territories governed by Signorie. The oppressive yoke that hung heavily upon these lands only deepened his appreciation for Florence's self-rule. It fueled his conviction to unravel the intricacies of power and governance, to decipher the underlying mechanisms that could ensure the survival and prosperity of a state.

Thus, within the fertile grounds of Lorenzo De Medici's enlightened Florence, Machiavelli's formative years germinated with the seeds of political insight. The city-state, prosperous and self-ruled, provided the perfect backdrop for him to delve into the intricate tapestry of governance, laying the foundation for his future contributions to political philosophy.

THE POLITICAL ODYSSEY: MACHIAVELLI'S TENURE AS CHANCELLOR AND SECRETARY, AND THE RESILIENCE OF HIS POLITICAL LEGACY

At the vibrant age of 29, when the world still shimmered with boundless possibilities, destiny beckoned to Niccolò Machiavelli with a proposition that would forever shape his political legacy. It was on that momentous day, the 14th of July in the year 1498, that he received a remarkable appointment that would launch him into the realm of power and governance. With great honor and responsibility, Machiavelli ascended to the coveted position of Chancellor and Secretary to the illustrious Dieci di Libertà e Pace, an esteemed council dedicated to preserving the liberties and peace of the republic.

For the next twelve years, Machiavelli dedicated his every waking hour to the arduous task of statecraft. As Chancellor and Secretary, he became a pivotal figure in the intricate machinery of governance, where his shrewd intellect and astute insights proved invaluable. With unwavering dedication, he delved into the complexities of diplomacy, meticulously crafting strategies and policies that safeguarded the republic's interests.

During his tenure, Machiavelli ceaselessly toiled, striving to ensure the prosperity and stability of the republic he held dear. His office became a beacon of tireless service, where his sharp mind dissected political machinations, his pen etching words of wisdom and guidance for the governance of the state. Within the hallowed halls of power, the controversial thinker of Florence navigated treacherous currents and intricate webs of influence, employing his keen perception to uphold the ideals of liberty and peace.

However, the winds of change are fickle, and the tides of political fortune can shift with capricious ease. In 1512, as the shadow of the De Medici family once again descended upon Florence, the republic's golden age reached its twilight. The fall of the republic marked the end of Machiavelli's political career, plunging him into the depths of uncertainty and disillusionment.

Though the De Medici family had regained their grasp on power, their reign proved to be short-lived. The seeds of Machiavelli's political insights and aspirations, sown during his time in office, would germinate and flourish in the coming years. For the indomitable spirit of a thinker like Machiavelli could not be quelled by the ebb and flow of political fortunes.

Thus, the chapter of Machiavelli's political life came to a close, but his legacy was far from extinguished. The fall of the republic marked not an end, but a transformation, as the seeds of his political philosophy took root in the depths of his mind. From the ashes of political disillusionment, he would emerge as a beacon of wisdom and guidance, shaping the course of political thought for generations to come.

JOURNEYS AND CHRONICLES: MACHIAVELLI'S PEN UNVEILING THE WORLD'S POLITICAL TAPESTRY

Throughout his illustrious political career, Niccolò Machiavelli embarked on numerous voyages that took him beyond the borders of his beloved Florence. These journeys served as catalysts for his intellectual growth, exposing him to diverse cultures and political landscapes. As he traversed the lands, his keen observations and insatiable curiosity compelled him to document his experiences in a myriad of writings.

Armed with a pen and an acute sense of perception, Machiavelli meticulously chronicled his encounters and reflections. His writings became tapestries woven with intricate details, capturing the essence of the foreign lands he explored. From the bustling streets of foreign cities to the courtly intrigues of distant realms, he crafted vivid portraits that resonated with readers for centuries to come.

In his writings, Machiavelli did not shy away from expressing his biting wit and sardonic humor. His notes brimmed with scathing satire, unveiling the follies and vices of those in positions of power. He wielded his pen like a rapier, exposing the hypocrisy and corruption that often tainted the political realm. His incisive commentary cut through the façades, revealing the harsh realities that lurked beneath the surface.

The depth and breadth of Machiavelli's writings were vast, and among his extensive repertoire were numerous pamphlets that have stood the test of time. These pamphlets, imbued with his trademark style, continue to be preserved in the annals of history, offering valuable insights into his political musings and perspectives.

From his travels and writings, Machiavelli gleaned invaluable lessons that shaped his political philosophy. The exposure to different governance systems and the scrutiny of rulers across borders expanded his understanding of the complexities of power. These experiences, coupled with his astute observations, formed the foundation of his groundbreaking work, "The Prince," and other renowned treatises.

DEFENDING THE REPUBLIC: MACHIAVELLI'S TRIUMPH IN ESTABLISHING FLORENCE'S NATIONAL MILITIA

In the early stages of his political career, Niccolò Machiavelli achieved a significant milestone that would leave an indelible mark on the history of Florence. Recognizing the inherent risks and limitations of relying on unreliable mercenary troops for the defense of the city-state, Machiavelli embarked on a mission to establish a National Militia, a force that would secure Florence's fortifications and protect its sovereignty.

With unwavering determination and political acumen, Machiavelli set out to persuade the authorities in Florence of the urgent need for change. Drawing upon his keen understanding of military affairs and his visionary insights, he presented a compelling case for the creation of a National Militia, a citizen-based force that would be dedicated to the defense of the republic.

Machiavelli's persuasive powers found an ally in the form of Piero Soderini, a renowned statesman and supporter of republicanism. Together, they rallied behind the cause, fervently advocating for the establishment of a new military system that would embody the spirit of civic duty and ensure the security of Florence.

Their efforts bore fruit, and Florence embraced the vision

put forth by Machiavelli and Soderini. The National Militia was born, an embodiment of civic pride and a symbol of the people's commitment to safeguarding their beloved city-state. This new military force, comprising ordinary citizens who were dedicated to the defense of their homeland, replaced the unreliable and costly mercenary troops that had previously served as the backbone of Florence's defense.

The establishment of the National Militia marked a watershed moment for Florence, heralding a new era of self-reliance and civic engagement. Machiavelli's vision of a citizen-led defense force not only enhanced the city-state's security but also fostered a sense of unity and collective responsibility among its inhabitants.

Under the guidance of Machiavelli and Soderini, the National Militia fortified Florence, ensuring its readiness to face any external threats. This accomplishment showcased the political theorist's ability to translate his visionary ideas into practical realities, transforming the military landscape of the republic.

In this pivotal achievement, the controversial figure exemplified his dedication to the well-being and autonomy of Florence. By advocating for the National Militia and successfully implementing this revolutionary military system, he demonstrated his unwavering commitment to the republic and its long-term prosperity.

Machiavelli's accomplishment in convincing Florence to discard unreliable mercenaries and establish a National Militia stands as a testament to his strategic thinking, political prowess, and unwavering belief in the power of citizen engagement. It was a landmark achievement that would shape not only the defense strategy of Florence but also leave a lasting legacy in the annals of military history and political thought.

UNVEILING THE POWER OF THE PEOPLE: HOW CATHERINA SFORZA INSPIRED MACHIAVELLI'S POLITICAL PHILOSOPHY IN 'THE PRINCE'

In 1499, Niccolò Machiavelli embarked on his first official mission that would leave an indelible mark on his political philosophy. His destination was the formidable Catherina Sforza, a woman of remarkable strength and resilience, who held the title of "my lady of Forlì" and became a source of inspiration for Machiavelli's renowned work, "The Prince."

As the Florentine political theorists ventured into the domain of Catherina Sforza, he witnessed firsthand her unwavering determination and her ability to navigate the treacherous political landscape of Forlì. What struck him most profoundly was her reliance on the confidence and support of the people rather than solely relying on the security of fortresses and military might.

From this encounter, Machiavelli gleaned a crucial moral lesson that would resonate throughout his political philosophy. He realized that true power and stability lie not in the physical fortifications of castles and strongholds, but in the hearts and minds of the people. The loyalty and trust of the populace, he concluded, were the cornerstones upon which lasting political success could be built.

In "The Prince," Machiavelli expounded upon this moral insight, advocating for rulers to prioritize the cultivation of the people's trust and support. He stressed the importance of fostering goodwill, maintaining a strong rapport with the citizenry, and employing strategies that would garner their confidence. He understood that the legitimacy and effectiveness of a leader's rule hinged upon the backing of the people, rather than mere reliance on physical defenses.

Through Catherina Sforza's example, Machiavelli recognized that the true essence of leadership lay in forging a symbiotic relationship with the governed. It was a departure from the conventional wisdom of his time, which emphasized the might of fortresses and the authority of rulers as the sole sources of power. He challenged the prevailing notions and championed a more nuanced understanding that placed the people at the center of political calculations.

In essence, Machiavelli's encounter with Catherina Sforza and his subsequent reflections served as a catalyst for his exploration of the delicate interplay between rulers and their subjects. His realization that the trust and support of the people were paramount to sustainable governance would shape his political thought, leaving an enduring legacy that would resonate throughout the centuries.

Indeed, inspired by the conduct of "my lady of Forlì," the father of modern political realism extracted a moral lesson that transcended the confines of their encounter. It became a cornerstone of his political philosophy, highlighting the significance of earning the confidence and loyalty of the people as a vital component of effective leadership, forever immortalized within the pages of "The Prince."

WHEN AMBITION MEETS REALITY: MACHIAVELLI'S REFLECTIONS ON THE FAILED FRENCH MISSION AND ITS INFLUENCE ON 'THE PRINCE'

In the year 1500, Niccolò Machiavelli embarked on a challenging mission to France with a crucial objective: to persuade King Louis XII to increase pressure on the ongoing invasion of Pisa. This mission represented a significant opportunity for the political theorist to showcase his diplomatic skills and negotiate in the interest of Florence. However, the outcome did not unfold as planned.

At the time, France's expansionist ambitions extended to Naples, and Machiavelli envisioned a grand strategy where the French would conquer more territories without a well-defined plan. However, this ambitious plan ultimately faltered, leading to a significant setback. As the French forces advanced further into Italian territories, they encountered numerous challenges and resistance from the locals. King Louis XII was compelled to negotiate and come to terms with the inhabitants, ultimately resulting in a defeat for the expansionist ambitions.

Machiavelli, ever the astute observer and analyst, thoroughly examined the failures and shortcomings of this endeavor. He delved into the intricacies of political and military strategy, dissecting the unforgivable errors committed during this campaign. These reflections and insights into the complexities of power, ambition, and the need for astute planning would later find their place in his masterpiece, "The Prince."

"The Prince," Machiavelli's renowned work on political philosophy, stands as a testament to his understanding of the intricacies and realities of political power. In this influential treatise, he explores the principles of effective leadership, drawing on historical examples and his own experiences. Through his analysis, Machiavelli seeks to provide guidance to rulers on how to attain and maintain power, avoiding pitfalls and learning from past mistakes.

The failed mission to France and the subsequent reflection on the errors committed played a significant role in shaping Machiavelli's thoughts and ideas as he penned "The Prince." His work serves as a pragmatic guide, urging rulers to navigate the complexities of politics with calculated strategies, adaptability, and a keen awareness of both their own interests and the prevailing circumstances.

Despite the setbacks and disappointments experienced during his diplomatic mission, Machiavelli's resilience and intellectual prowess allowed him to transform these experiences into valuable insights that would continue to resonate through the ages. His dedication to understanding the realities of political power and his willingness to confront the harsh truths of human nature remain enduring legacies of his work.

MACHIAVELLI'S TRAGIC FATE: FROM IMPRISONMENT TO EXILE, THE DEMISE OF A POLITICAL THINKER

Following the reinstatement of the Medici family in Florence, Niccolò Machiavelli faced a tumultuous and unfortunate turn of events. Suspected of involvement in a conspiracy against the ruling power, he was subjected to imprisonment and torture. However, due to a lack of substantial evidence, he was eventually released from custody. Despite his efforts to appease the Medici family through an overly effusive tone and a dedication in his work, Machiavelli did not regain their favor.

Hoping for a return to his previous position in the government, Machiavelli's expectations were shattered when it became clear that his political career had come to an abrupt end. Confined to his estate, he found himself isolated from the world he once navigated with skill and ambition. The disappointment and disillusionment that followed this dramatic fall from grace weighed heavily on him.

Sadly, his exile and the loss of his political influence took a toll on his health. Just a month after his confinement, he passed away, leaving behind a legacy that would endure through his writings but with a sense of unfulfilled potential. His death marked the end of a turbulent and eventful life, a life dedicated to the pursuit of political knowledge and the advancement of his beloved Florence.

The circumstances surrounding Machiavelli's incarceration, torture, and subsequent exile reflect the volatile and unpredictable nature of political power during that era. Despite his efforts to align himself with the ruling family, his previous associations and his own political writings likely contributed to his downfall. Nevertheless, his enduring contributions to political thought and his reputation as a keen observer of human nature continue to shape our understanding of politics and leadership to this day.

THE PRINCE: FROM FORBIDDEN MANUSCRIPT TO POLITICAL PHENOMENON, MACHIAVELLI'S CONTROVERSIAL MAGNUM OPUS LEAVES A LASTING IMPRESSION

In 1532, "The Prince" by Niccolò Machiavelli was published under the order of Pope Clement VII. This publication marked the beginning of a remarkable journey for Machiavelli's seminal work, which would ultimately become both revered and reviled in the political landscape of its time.

Initially intended as a practical guide for rulers, "The Prince" garnered attention from political figures across Europe. Its astute analysis of power dynamics, unflinching realism, and pragmatic approach to governance captured the imagination of many leaders seeking to strengthen their rule. The book quickly found its way into the hands of those in positions of influence, who eagerly absorbed its teachings and sought to implement its strategies.

However, the controversial nature of "The Prince" would not

escape the scrutiny of religious and political authorities. Less than twenty years after its publication, the book was included in the list of forbidden books, indicating that its content clashed with the prevailing religious and moral norms of the time. The Church, concerned about the potentially subversive implications of the controversial thinker's ideas, sought to suppress the dissemination of the text.

Nonetheless, the allure of Machiavelli's work proved too strong to resist, even in the face of official censure. Despite being labeled as forbidden, "The Prince" continued to circulate clandestinely among political circles, with many figures clandestinely acquiring copies and studying its contents. The book's reputation as a shrewd and incisive manual for acquiring and maintaining power ensured its enduring relevance in the corridors of influence.

"The Prince" became a secret weapon for ambitious rulers, who saw in its pages a roadmap to success in the complex world of politics. Its teachings were often interpreted, sometimes even twisted, to justify morally questionable actions and manipulate the political landscape to one's advantage. Machiavelli's work, originally intended as a pragmatic guide, was now being used and abused for personal and political gain.

The paradoxical status of "The Prince" as a forbidden text that exerted a profound influence on political thought highlights its enduring significance. Despite attempts to suppress it, the book managed to permeate the intellectual and political zeitgeist of the time. Its controversial reputation and the allure of its Machiavellian principles ensured its place as a touchstone for future generations of politicians and scholars alike.

Today, "The Prince" stands as a testament to the enduring impact of the diplomat and historian's ideas. It serves as a reminder of the complex relationship between power, morality, and the pursuit of political goals. While its legacy is marred by abuse and manipulation, its insights continue to stimulate critical discourse on the nature of leadership, the dynamics of power, and the complexities of governance.

PRAGMATIC PRINCIPLES OF GOVERNANCE: MACHIAVELLI'S INSIGHTS ON EFFECTIVE RULE EXPLORED IN THE OPENING CHAPTER OF 'THE PRINCE'

The opening chapter of "The Prince" indeed establishes a tone of pragmatic political advice, reflecting Niccolò Machiavelli's common-sense approach to governance. In this chapter, the man who changed the way we think about politics emphasizes several key principles for effective rule, providing insights that still resonate today.

One of the fundamental principles highlighted by Machiavelli is the importance of a ruler's physical presence within their principality. He asserts that rulers should reside in the territories they govern, actively engaging with their subjects and being accessible to them. This hands-on approach allows for better understanding of the needs and concerns of the people, enabling more effective governance.

He also advises against excessive reliance on colonies, cautioning rulers to spend little or no resources on establishing and maintaining distant territories. Instead, he advocates for the focus to be on consolidating power and strengthening the core territory. This pragmatic approach recognizes the potential pitfalls and challenges associated with expansive colonial endeavors.

In terms of military strategy, Machiavelli expresses reservations about relying heavily on mercenaries, emphasizing the importance of building a dependable cavalry composed of warriors preferably drawn from the ruler's own city. This emphasis on local warriors highlights Machiavelli's belief in the loyalty and commitment that can be fostered among those who have a direct stake in the defense and well-being of their own community.

It is notable that the Renaissance thinker displays skepticism toward the effectiveness of firearms during his time. Instead, he places value on well-trained foot soldiers, considering them a valuable asset for territorial defense. This perspective underscores his belief in the importance of disciplined and skilled warriors who can effectively protect and assert control over a principality.

Additionally, Machiavelli warns against rulers isolating themselves within fortresses. He emphasizes the need for rulers to maintain a connection with their subjects, engaging in dialogue and remaining visible. Isolation, in his view, can breed mistrust and detachment, potentially undermining a ruler's authority and effectiveness.

These principles, outlined in the first chapter of "The Prince," reflect Machiavelli's pragmatic approach to governance. They highlight his belief in the importance of personal presence, strategic military choices, and the need for rulers to remain connected to their subjects. While some aspects may reflect the historical context of Machiavelli's time, the underlying principles continue to offer valuable insights into effective leadership and governance in the present day.

UNDERSTANDING MACHIAVELLI'S PERSPECTIVE ON CONQUERED TERRITORIES IN 'THE PRINCE'

Indeed, in the section on principalities in "The Prince," Machiavelli presents a pragmatic perspective on maintaining order in conquered cities and territories. While he suggests that one potential strategy is to destroy them, it is important to understand the context and nuances of his argument.

His view on the destruction of conquered cities stems from his analysis of historical examples and the challenges faced by rulers in maintaining control over newly acquired territories. He argues that if a ruler finds it necessary to subdue a rebellious city or territory, it may be more effective to employ drastic measures, including destruction, rather than attempting to govern through leniency alone.

Machiavelli's rationale behind this approach is rooted in his understanding of human nature and the dynamics of power. He believed that conquered territories, particularly those with a history of resistance or rebellion, were prone to conspiracies and uprisings. To mitigate these risks and establish a sense of order, Machiavelli argues that rulers should consider employing decisive actions that serve as a deterrent and discourage future challenges to their authority.

However, it is crucial to note that the Italian statesman does not advocate for the wholesale destruction of all conquered territories. His argument is based on a pragmatic evaluation of specific circumstances and the potential benefits of employing strong measures in certain cases. He emphasizes the importance of understanding the context, weighing the costs and benefits, and making calculated decisions based on the unique dynamics of each situation.

Machiavelli's exploration of conspiracy in "The Prince" reflects his astute understanding of the political landscape and the challenges faced by rulers in maintaining stability and control. He acknowledges the presence of conspiratorial tendencies in human nature and advises rulers to be vigilant, employing strategies to detect and neutralize potential threats to their rule.

It is worth noting that his approach to governance, including his perspective on the destruction of conquered territories and the theory of conspiracy, has been a subject of much debate and interpretation. Some argue that his ideas were a reflection of the harsh realities of his time, while others view them as a thought-provoking exploration of the complexities of political power and the lengths to which leaders must go to maintain control.

Ultimately, Machiavelli's insights on these subjects challenge conventional notions of governance and invite readers to critically examine the practical dilemmas faced by rulers in their quest for stability and control.

THE INTRIGUING INFLUENCE OF CESARE BORGIA: UNRAVELING MACHIAVELLI'S INSPIRATION IN 'THE PRINCE'

Inspired by the rise and fall of Cesare Borgia, critics argue that Niccolò Machiavelli found intrigue in his tumultuous life, which served as a source of inspiration for his writings. Cesare Borgia, often referred to as the Duke Valentine, was the son of Pope Alexander VI and achieved significant notoriety for his captivating persona as a condottiero, or military leader, before becoming a central figure in Machiavelli's book.

Cesare Borgia's story is marked by a complex mixture of fortune and infamy. At a young age, he was elevated to the position of cardinal by his father, which provided him with considerable influence and opportunities. However, Cesare's life was characterized by a rapid descent into a world of vices and debauchery. He was known for his brutal nature and his propensity for silence, which instilled fear in those around him.

Tragically, Cesare's life came to a premature end during a street fight in Austria. His mutilated body was discovered unclothed in a corner, leaving those who found him unaware of his true identity. This mysterious and grisly end added an air of intrigue to the already captivating tale of Cesare Borgia.

Machiavelli's fascination with Cesare Borgia lies in the complex nature of his character and his swift rise and fall from power. Borgia's ruthless approach to achieving and maintaining control, combined with his enigmatic persona, made him a figure of great interest for Machiavelli's exploration of political dynamics and the pursuit of power.

Critics argue that Borgia's story served as a foundation for Machiavelli's conceptualization of a successful ruler in "The Prince." While Machiavelli does not explicitly mention Borgia by name in the book, his depiction of an astute and adaptive leader who utilizes both force and cunning aligns with the characteristics often attributed to Borgia.

It is important to note, however, that the author of 'The Prince' utilization of Borgia's story is not meant to be a glorification of his actions or an endorsement of his behavior. Instead, Borgia's life serves as a cautionary tale, highlighting the complexities and challenges faced by leaders in their pursuit and exercise of power.

The enigmatic figure of Cesare Borgia continues to captivate scholars and readers alike, and his presence in Machiavelli's work adds depth and intrigue to the exploration of political philosophy and the quest for effective leadership.

UNWAVERING INTEGRITY: MACHIAVELLI'S REFLECTION ON LOYALTY AND HONESTY IN HIS POLITICAL CAREER

Embedded within Niccolò Machiavelli's reflections on his 12-year tenure as a public servant lies a passage that reads almost like a purification, a reaffirmation of his unwavering loyalty and integrity. He unequivocally asserts, "And of my loyalty none could doubt, because having always kept faith I could not now learn how to break it." These words serve as a testament to his steadfast commitment to honor and trustworthiness, values deeply ingrained within him.

The diplomat, aware of the controversies and complexities surrounding his political career, emphasizes that his unwavering faithfulness was an integral part of his nature. He firmly believed that one's character remains consistent over time, and his own consistent demonstration of fidelity served as irrefutable evidence of his unyielding integrity.

In a poignant reflection, Machiavelli draws a connection between his poverty and his honesty, presenting it as a testament to his virtuous conduct. His modest circumstances serve as a tangible testament to the absence of ill-gotten gains or corrupt practices, reinforcing the notion that his loyalty and honesty were unwavering despite the challenges he faced.

This passage allows us to glimpse into the political theorist's moral compass and the principles that guided his actions. It showcases his unyielding commitment to upholding his values and remaining true to his word, even in the face of adversity and the temptations of power.

The words resonate as a reminder that integrity and fidelity are qualities that should endure throughout one's life, regardless of the circumstances. Machiavelli's affirmation of his own steadfastness serves as an implicit call for others to uphold similar virtues, to remain resolute in their commitments, and to let their actions speak for their character.

In this passage, we witness a deeply introspective Machiavelli, offering a glimpse into the motivations and convictions that shaped his political career. It is a moment of self-reflection, a declaration of personal values, and a resolute affirmation of his unbreakable commitment to loyalty and honesty.

These words resonate beyond the context of the Italian statesman's own experiences, serving as a timeless reminder of the importance of unwavering principles, ethical conduct, and the enduring power of one's character. They invite us to reflect on our own actions and the choices we make, encouraging us to embody loyalty and honesty in all aspects of our lives.

MACHIAVELLI'S PARADOX: UNVEILING THE CONSERVATISM IN HIS REVOLUTIONARY POLITICAL THOUGHT

In his masterpiece, he revolutionized the study of politics, transforming it into a discipline informed by modern sensibilities. Yet, beneath the progressive veneer of his writings, Machiavelli's political disposition remained rooted in a deep-seated conservatism.

Machiavelli dissected the intricate dynamics of power, unabashedly exposing the machinations employed by rulers to secure and maintain their dominance. His work resonated with readers precisely because it departed from the conventional wisdom of his time. Machiavelli discarded the idealistic notions of politics and instead examined the raw realities of human nature and the pragmatic strategies employed by leaders to navigate the treacherous waters of governance.

However, while his approach may have seemed radical and modern for its time, it is important to recognize the undercurrent of conservatism that shaped his thinking. Rooted in a deep reverence for stability, order, and the preservation of established hierarchies, Machiavelli's political philosophy displayed a conservative outlook.

He believed in the inherent frailties of human nature,

advocating for leaders to be guided by realism rather than lofty ideals. The controversial figure of Florence emphasized the necessity of strong leadership, arguing that rulers should prioritize the security and stability of the state over individual liberties or democratic principles. He recognized the need for a firm hand at the helm, embracing the notion that the ends can sometimes justify the means.

Machiavelli's conservatism was also evident in his deep admiration for ancient Rome and its republican values. He drew inspiration from the Roman Republic, seeing it as a model of stability and virtue. Machiavelli revered the Roman commitment to order, discipline, and the rule of law, often contrasting it with what he perceived as the chaotic and turbulent state of his contemporary Italy.

Thus, while Machiavelli's writings ushered in a new era of political thought with their modern language and realistic approach, his underlying conservatism cannot be overlooked. He sought to strike a delicate balance between acknowledging the realities of power and preserving the stability and hierarchical order of the state.

It is this fusion of modernity and conservatism that makes Machiavelli's contributions to political science so profound. His willingness to confront uncomfortable truths and challenge conventional wisdom paved the way for a more nuanced understanding of politics. By embracing the complexities of human nature and the need for effective leadership, Machiavelli's legacy continues to shape the study of politics and inspire critical inquiry into the delicate dance between power, stability, and governance.

"The Prince" was indeed written with the intention of serving as a manual in the realm of political science, a guidebook for rulers navigating the treacherous terrain of power. At its core, the book proposes that leaders must be prepared to take any necessary actions, regardless of their moral implications, to protect themselves and secure their position in a world filled with potential adversaries.

The Renaissance thinker's perspective, as expressed in "The Prince," is one of pragmatic realism, urging leaders to be astute observers of human nature and to adapt their strategies accordingly. He argues that leaders must be willing to employ both virtuous and, if necessary, unscrupulous means to achieve their goals and maintain their authority. In this sense, Machiavelli's doctrine is marked by a willingness to set aside traditional moral constraints in the pursuit of political survival and success.

While he acknowledges that certain actions may be considered morally questionable, he posits that their justification lies in their utility and effectiveness in safeguarding the leader's position. According to his perspective, if a particular action serves the purpose of self-defense, consolidation of power, or the preservation of the state, it can be deemed justifiable, regardless of its inherent ethical implications.

The writer's stance challenges conventional moral frameworks and places emphasis on practicality and expediency in the realm of politics. This approach has sparked intense debate and controversy over the centuries, with some viewing it as an amoral endorsement of Machiavellian tactics, while others interpret it as a realistic assessment of the complexities of political power.

It is important to note, however, that Machiavelli's teachings should not be taken in isolation or as a complete guide to ethical leadership. His ideas, while provocative, need to be considered within the historical and political context in which they were formulated.

Ultimately, "The Prince" serves as a thought-provoking exploration of power dynamics and political strategies. It challenges conventional notions of morality and raises important questions about the nature of leadership and the choices leaders face in the pursuit of their objectives. It is a text that continues to spark discussion and debate, compelling us to critically examine the relationship between power, ethics, and the practical realities of political governance.

THE ENIGMATIC DEDICATION: UNRAVELING THE FATE OF MACHIAVELLI'S 'THE LITTLE BOOK' AND ITS PATRON

"The Little Book," as it was initially referred to during its development, underwent various transformations in terms of its patron and title. Niccolò Machiavelli's work experienced a series of shifts and dedications, ultimately culminating in its dedication to Piero Lorenzo De Medici, the grandson of Lorenzo. However, the reception of the book by Lorenzo and its ultimate fate remain shrouded in uncertainty.

Throughout the process of writing and refining his manuscript, Machiavelli sought the support and patronage of influential figures to enhance its credibility and dissemination. As he revised and shaped his ideas, different patrons were considered, and the title of the work evolved in tandem with these shifts. "The Little Book" served as a provisional designation, subject to change as its intended audience and purpose became clearer.

In the end, the diplomat chose to dedicate the book to Piero Lorenzo De Medici, the grandson of Lorenzo De Medici, also known as Lorenzo the Magnificent. This decision reflected Machiavelli's desire to align himself with the prestigious Medici family, which held considerable political power and influence in Florence and beyond. By associating his work with a member of the Medici dynasty, Machiavelli sought to secure their patronage and gain favor in the political landscape.

However, the extent to which Lorenzo De Medici received or engaged with "The Little Book" remains a mystery. It is unknown whether Lorenzo ever received it as a gift or had the opportunity to read its contents. The complexities of political intrigue and the changing tides of fortune may have played a role in determining the book's reception by its intended dedicatee.

The uncertainty surrounding Lorenzo's reception of "The Little Book" does not diminish its significance. Despite any potential lack of direct acknowledgment from its dedicated patron, the work itself went on to become a landmark in political philosophy. Its ideas and principles continue to resonate and shape political discourse, regardless of the specific circumstances of its dedication.

The dedication to Piero Lorenzo De Medici, while potentially symbolic, underscores the interplay between politics and intellectual pursuits during Machiavelli's time. It highlights the delicate balance between seeking patronage and expressing one's ideas freely, often requiring strategic decisions to navigate the complex dynamics of the era.

In the end, whether Lorenzo received "The Little Book" as a gift or read its contents is a mystery that remains buried in history. Nonetheless, the enduring legacy of the work, now known as "The Prince," transcends any uncertainties surrounding its reception. Its impact on political thought and its enduring relevance in the realms of governance and leadership persist, cementing its status as a seminal text in the annals of political philosophy.

DEBATES AND DISPUTES: THE AUTHORSHIP MYSTERY OF MACHIAVELLI'S 'THE PRINCE'

During Niccolò Machiavelli's lifetime, there were accusations and controversies surrounding the authorship and publication of "The Prince." These disputes cast doubt on its origins and raised questions about its authenticity. Some critics claimed that the political theorist of Florence did not write the book and that it was plagiarized from other sources. These controversies have persisted over time, leading to ongoing debates and disputes regarding the true authorship and textual integrity of "The Prince."

One of the main factors contributing to the disputes surrounding "The Prince" is the absence of Machiavelli's direct acknowledgment of authorship. Unlike his other works, Machiavelli did not include his name as the author of "The Prince" when it was published. This omission gave rise to speculation and fueled the allegations of plagiarism and unauthorized publication.

Additionally, the nature of "The Prince" itself, with its bold and controversial ideas, led some critics to question whether Machiavelli could have been the true author. The Machiavellian principles outlined in the book, advocating for the pursuit and maintenance of power through strategic means, were considered unorthodox and contrary to traditional moral and political norms of the time. This further fueled skepticism regarding Machiavelli's authorship.

Moreover, the lack of definitive manuscripts or original texts authored by Machiavelli himself adds to the disputability of the 'little book.' Various editions and translations of the book exist, each with potential variations and inconsistencies. Scholars and historians have devoted considerable effort to analyzing and comparing these different versions, attempting to discern the most accurate representation of Machiavelli's original work.

The disputes surrounding the authorship and text of his work persist to this day. Scholars and experts continue to engage in rigorous textual analysis and scholarly debates in an attempt to unravel the truth and determine the extent of the historian's involvement in the book's creation. While some maintain that Machiavelli authored the work, others argue that it was a collaborative effort or a compilation of existing ideas.

Regardless of these disputes, it is undeniable that the literary masterpiece has had a profound impact on political thought and continues to be studied and debated by scholars, politicians, and thinkers around the world. Its enduring legacy lies in its provocative and influential ideas, which have shaped discussions on power, governance, and leadership for centuries.

THE FATHER OF MODERN POLITICAL SCIENCE'S LITERARY MUSE: THE PROFOUND INFLUENCE OF DANTE ALIGHIERI ON THE POLITICAL THINKER

Machiavelli held the renowned poet and statesman Dante Alighieri in high regard, considering him as one of his heroes and a source of inspiration. Many scholars have observed Machiavelli's attempts to emulate Dante's style and literary techniques in his own writings. In particular, there is one passage where Machiavelli quotes Dante, albeit with a translation that may not capture the full essence of the original Italian text.

However, it is worth noting that Machiavelli's admiration for Dante extended beyond mere imitation of his writing style. Dante's political ideas and philosophical concepts, as showcased in his epic work "The Divine Comedy," greatly influenced Machiavelli's own political thought. Machiavelli saw Dante as a symbol of political wisdom and a voice that transcended his time, providing invaluable insights into the complexities of governance and the nature of power.

By drawing inspiration from Dante, the Italian political theorist sought to infuse his own works with the depth, symbolism, and allegorical richness for which Dante was renowned. He recognized the power of literature and rhetoric in conveying complex political ideas and aimed to harness those tools to communicate his own theories effectively.

Machiavelli's admiration for Dante's poetic and political genius serves as a testament to the interplay between literature and politics during the Renaissance era. It highlights the way in which thinkers and writers of the time drew inspiration from one another, building upon the works of their predecessors to shape their own contributions to the intellectual landscape.

While the writer of 'The Prince' sought to follow in Dante's footsteps and emulate his style, he also carved out his own unique path, becoming a prominent political philosopher in his own right. By combining his observations of historical events and his astute understanding of human nature, Machiavelli forged a distinct approach to political thought that continues to be studied and debated to this day.

In essence, his affinity for Dante Alighieri speaks to his deep appreciation for the intertwining realms of literature, politics, and philosophy. It underscores the enduring influence of Dante's works and the profound impact they had on shaping the intellectual development of subsequent thinkers, including Machiavelli himself.

MACHIAVELLI'S COMPLEX VIEW OF FRA SAVONAROLA: EXPLORING THE INTERSECTION OF MORALITY AND POLITICAL STRATEGY

Niccolò Machiavelli held a complex view of Fra Savonarola, a prominent Dominican friar who rose to political prominence in Florence after 1494. While Machiavelli was critical of certain aspects of Savonarola's approach, he also recognized and admired his oratorical skills. According to Machiavelli, the downfall of the unarmed prophet was primarily attributed to his lack of military strategy and political experience.

Savonarola emerged as a charismatic figure during a period of political and social upheaval in Florence. His fiery sermons and calls for moral and religious reform resonated with many Florentines, leading to a significant following and a temporary shift in the city's political landscape. However, The diplomat, a keen observer of politics, identified certain weaknesses in Savonarola's approach.

While Machiavelli acknowledged Savonarola's impressive oratory skills, he believed that the friar's political influence ultimately faltered due to his inability to navigate the intricate world of military strategy and governance. The acute thinker, who emphasized the importance of pragmatic decision-making and effective leadership, saw Savonarola's lack of experience in these areas as a significant factor contributing to his downfall.

Machiavelli's perspective suggests that political success requires more than just charisma and moral fervor. It demands an understanding of the practical realities of power, including military strength, diplomatic maneuvering, and strategic thinking. From his vantage point, Savonarola's inability to adapt his approach to the challenges of political governance left him vulnerable and ultimately contributed to his loss of influence.

It is important to note that Machiavelli's assessment of Savonarola was influenced by his own pragmatic worldview and his belief in the necessity of political astuteness. However, it is also worth recognizing that Machiavelli himself had his own criticisms of the ruling elites and religious institutions of his time, which he expressed in his writings.

In examining the Italian diplomat's view of Savonarola, we gain insight into the complexities of political dynamics and the factors that contribute to success or failure in the realm of governance. It highlights the tension between idealism and practicality, between moral conviction and political maneuvering, which Machiavelli sought to navigate and understand in his own exploration of political philosophy.

THE CHURCH'S ROLE IN ITALY: MACHIAVELLI'S CRITIQUE AND THE QUEST FOR UNITY

Within the depths of Niccolò Machiavelli's political musings, one finds a critical assessment of the role of the Church in the affairs of Italy. Machiavelli perceived that the Church wielded an overwhelming influence, and he believed this influence to be a significant factor contributing to Italy's woes. In his writings, he lamented the state of piety and religion, contending that Italy had lost its spiritual compass and suffered from a lack of unity.

He observed that the priests of Rome, who were expected to guide and unite the Italian states, fell short of their responsibilities. In his view, they lacked the strength and authority necessary to govern and bring about a sense of cohesion among the diverse regions of Italy. Instead of fostering unity, the Church became entangled in its own struggles for power and influence, further exacerbating the divisions within the country.

For the father of modern political science, the absence of a unifying force was a cause for concern. He questioned the state of Italy's collective identity, pointing to the fragmented nature of the various states and the absence of a shared purpose. In his writings, he yearned for a sense of unity that would transcend regional boundaries and enable Italy to stand strong against external threats.

While Machiavelli recognized the historical and cultural significance of the Church, his critique centered on what he perceived as its failure to fulfill its role as a unifying force. He criticized the Church's weak leadership, viewing it as a hindrance to the consolidation of power and the establishment of a strong and prosperous Italy.

In questioning the Church's influence and highlighting the lack of unity, the Italian statesman opened a dialogue on the need for strong secular leadership and a clear vision for the nation. His reflections laid the groundwork for his political philosophy, emphasizing the importance of effective governance, the consolidation of power, and the pursuit of national interests.

It is essential to contextualize Machiavelli's views within the political and social climate of his time. The Church's involvement in politics and the complexities of Italy's regional rivalries provided fertile ground for his observations and criticisms. Machiavelli's questioning of the Church's influence, coupled with his call for unity, represented a departure from the prevailing norms and a plea for a more coherent and robust Italian state.

The author's writings, while controversial in their time, continue to provoke intellectual discourse and inspire critical examination of the role of religion and governance in society. His reflections on the Church's influence and the need for unity serve as a testament to his unwavering commitment to Italy's well-being and his quest for a stronger, more cohesive nation.

THE COMPLEX APPROACH: MACHIAVELLI'S CHALLENGE TO THE LINK BETWEEN MORALITY AND GLORY IN POLITICS

Machiavelli's thought often challenged the prevailing beliefs of his time, and one such belief he questioned was the humanist notion that glory and virtue are inherently linked. He expressed a skeptical view regarding the direct correlation between virtuous actions and the attainment of glory or success. According to the controversial figure of Florence, it is not always rational to prioritize morality in the pursuit of political power or personal ambitions.

In his analysis of politics and leadership, Machiavelli recognized that the world is often governed by complex dynamics and practical considerations that may deviate from traditional moral principles. He believed that leaders must navigate the intricate web of human interactions and power struggles, where moral actions alone may not always yield the desired outcomes.

His perspective on morality in politics can be understood in the context of his emphasis on pragmatism and the realpolitik approach. He argued that leaders should prioritize the preservation and consolidation of their power and the well-being of their state or principality, even if it meant making choices that would be considered morally questionable by conventional standards.

While Machiavelli did not advocate for immoral or unethical behavior for its own sake, he argued that leaders should be willing to employ both virtuous and non-virtuous means, depending on the circumstances, to achieve their objectives. He believed that leaders must be adaptable and willing to make calculated decisions that may deviate from traditional moral norms in order to secure and maintain their positions of power.

It is important to note that the theorist's views on morality and politics have been a subject of debate and interpretation over the centuries. Some critics perceive his perspective as amoral or even immoral, while others argue that he provided a realistic assessment of the complexities of political life.

Machiavelli's assertion that it is not always rational to prioritize morality reflects his pragmatic approach to politics and his recognition of the multifaceted nature of human behavior and ambition. It serves as a reminder that the pursuit of power and success often necessitates difficult choices and trade-offs that may challenge conventional moral principles.

Indeed, he emphasized the importance of avoiding extreme approaches in politics, namely pure force and pure fraud. In his writings, he offered guidance on how rulers should navigate the intricate realm of politics without resorting solely to brute force or deceit.

Machiavelli understood that excessive reliance on force could lead to instability, resentment, and potential rebellion among the people. While he acknowledged the necessity of maintaining a strong military and the occasional use of force to protect the state's interests, he cautioned against the indiscriminate and unchecked use of power. Machiavelli believed that rulers should strive to establish a balance between assertiveness and restraint, ensuring that force is employed judiciously and in the best interest of the state.

Similarly, the father of political realisms cautioned against excessive reliance on fraud and deception as a means of achieving and maintaining power. While he recognized the role of strategic maneuvering and calculated actions in politics, he cautioned against relying solely on deceitful practices that could erode trust and undermine stability. Machiavelli emphasized the importance of cultivating a reputation for reliability and integrity, as leaders who are seen as trustworthy and honorable are more likely to garner support and loyalty.

For the Italian thinker, successful political leadership required a nuanced and strategic approach. He advocated for a blend of prudence, wisdom, and practicality. A ruler should be astute in understanding the motivations and desires of those they govern, adept at navigating complex political landscapes, and capable of employing a range of tools and strategies to achieve their objectives while minimizing the negative consequences.

By cautioning against pure force and pure fraud, the Florentine adviser sought to encourage leaders to consider the long-term implications of their actions and to recognize that effective governance requires a delicate balance between strength and subtlety.

UNVEILING THE LAYERS OF INTERPRETATION: DECODING MACHIAVELLI'S IDEAS ON POWER, MORALITY, AND POLITICS

Machiavelli's ideas have been subject to various layers of interpretation throughout history, reflecting the complexity and depth of his works. These interpretations have been influenced by the socio-political context of different periods and the lenses through which scholars and thinkers have approached his writings. Here are a few notable layers of interpretation applied to Machiavelli's ideas:

1. Realism vs. Idealism: One significant layer of interpretation revolves around the question of whether Machiavelli's writings should be seen as a realistic analysis of political power or as a prescription for ideal political behavior. Some view Machiavelli as a realist who provided pragmatic advice on how leaders should navigate the complexities of power, while others argue that his works were intended to inspire ideal political systems or provoke critical thinking.

2. Amorality vs. Morality: Another layer of interpretation focuses on the moral implications of Machiavelli's ideas. Critics often highlight the perceived amoral nature of his writings,

emphasizing his endorsement of actions that may be considered morally questionable. Others argue that the acute thinker of Florence aimed to reconcile moral and political concerns, recognizing the need for leaders to adapt their actions to the political realities they face.

3. Power and Ethics: Machiavelli's views on power and ethics have sparked considerable debate. Some interpretations emphasize the notion that the pursuit and maintenance of power are central concerns for political leaders, often leading to compromises in ethical behavior. Others explore the ethical implications of his writings, considering how the Italian statesman grappled with the tension between the pursuit of power and the moral responsibilities of rulers.

4. Historical Context: Understanding the historical context in which Machiavelli wrote is crucial to interpreting his ideas. His works emerged during a time of political turmoil in Italy, and he drew inspiration from historical events and figures. Interpreters often examine the political climate of the Renaissance, the rise of powerful city-states, and the power struggles among Italian princes to gain insight into Machiavelli's perspectives.

5. Influence and Reception: The layer of interpretation focusing on Machiavelli's influence and reception explores how his ideas have resonated over time and their impact on subsequent political thought. Scholars examine how his works shaped political discourse, influenced political theorists, and even influenced real-world leaders in their decision-making processes.

These layers of interpretation demonstrate the richness and complexity of Machiavelli's ideas. They highlight the enduring relevance of his works and the ongoing dialogue surrounding the nature of power, leadership, and ethics in politics. The Florentine political philosopher's writings continue to provoke thoughtful analysis and offer valuable insights into the complexities of political behavior and governance.

APPLYING MACHIAVELLI'S DOCTRINE TO MODERN POLITICS: NAVIGATING POWER AND STRATEGY IN A COMPLEX WORLD

Yes, Machiavelli's doctrine can be incorporated into today's political strategy, although it is important to approach it with caution and adapt it to the specific context and ethical considerations of contemporary politics. The Italian statesman's teachings emphasize the pragmatic realities of power and offer insights into effective leadership and governance. Here are a few key aspects of Machiavelli's doctrine that can be relevant in modern political strategy:

1. Realism and Practicality: Machiavelli's perspective emphasizes a realistic understanding of politics, recognizing that leaders must navigate complex power dynamics and make tough decisions based on practical considerations rather than idealistic notions. This approach can help policymakers assess the feasibility and consequences of their actions, considering the interests and motivations of various stakeholders.

2. Understanding Human Nature: Machiavelli's insights into human nature, particularly the inherent self-interest and ambition of individuals, can inform strategies for building

alliances, managing conflicts, and motivating political actors. Recognizing the motivations and behaviors of different individuals and groups allows policymakers to anticipate and respond to political challenges effectively.

3. Flexibility and Adaptability: Machiavelli stresses the importance of adaptability in politics. Circumstances change, and leaders must be willing to adjust their strategies accordingly. This involves being open to new information, being willing to revise plans, and seizing opportunities as they arise.

4. Prudent Use of Power: The influential Florentine figure encourages leaders to be firm and assertive in exercising power when necessary, but also cautions against excessive cruelty or abuse. Leaders should be mindful of how their actions are perceived by the public and the long-term implications of their decisions. Prudent and strategic use of power can help maintain stability and achieve policy goals.

However, it is crucial to approach Machiavelli's doctrine ethically and within the boundaries of legal and democratic norms. While his teachings offer insights into political strategy, they should not be used as a justification for unethical or immoral behavior. Modern political leaders need to balance realism with ethical considerations, ensuring that their actions align with democratic values, human rights, and the well-being of their constituents.

Indeed, political strategies should also incorporate other perspectives and theories from various fields such as ethics, economics, sociology, and international relations. Machiavelli's perspective can be a valuable tool in the political strategist's toolbox, but it should be employed alongside other theories and frameworks to develop a comprehensive and balanced approach to modern governance.

SUMMARY OF KEY CONCEPTS

1. Machiavellianism: Refers to the political philosophy and principles associated with Niccolò Machiavelli, particularly his pragmatic approach to power, morality, and leadership.

2. Pragmatic Realism: Machiavelli's perspective that political leaders should prioritize practicality and effectiveness over idealistic notions of morality, advocating for strategies and actions that maintain and strengthen their power.

3. Ends Justify the Means: Machiavelli's controversial belief that the desired outcome or goal justifies the methods used to achieve it, even if those methods are morally questionable or ethically compromising.

4. Virtù: Machiavelli's concept of virtue, which goes beyond conventional notions of morality. Virtù refers to qualities such as strength, cunning, and strategic thinking that enable leaders to navigate the complexities of politics and maintain their rule.

5. Influence and Interpretation: The impact of Machiavelli's ideas on political theory, philosophy, and governance throughout history. Various thinkers and leaders have interpreted and adapted his concepts to suit their own contexts, leading to diverse perspectives on Machiavellian principles.

6. Critiques and Challenges: Examination and criticism of Machiavelli's philosophy, particularly regarding its perceived lack of ethical considerations and potential dangers of unrestrained

power. Debates arise around the compatibility of Machiavellian principles with democratic values and the potential for abuse.

7. Contemporary Relevance: Exploration of the relevance of Machiavelli's ideas in modern politics, international relations, and management. The application and adaptation of his principles in different contexts and their implications for governance and leadership today.

These key concepts provide a foundation for understanding Machiavelli's political philosophy, its historical significance, ongoing debates, and its enduring relevance in the study of politics and power dynamics.

BIBLIOGRAPHY

1. Machiavelli, Niccolò. "The Prince." Translated by W. K. Marriott, Public Domain Books, 2021.

2. Mansfield, Harvey C. "Machiavelli's Virtue." University of Chicago Press, 1996.

3. Skinner, Quentin. "Machiavelli: A Very Short Introduction." Oxford University Press, 2000.

4. Gilbert, Felix. "Machiavelli and Guicciardini: Politics and History in Sixteenth-Century Florence." Princeton University Press, 2014.

5. Viroli, Maurizio. "Niccolò's Smile: A Biography of Machiavelli." Hill and Wang, 2000.

6. Boucher, David. "Political Theories of International Relations: From Thucydides to the Present." Oxford University Press, 2012.

7. Parel, Anthony. "The Political Calculus: Essays on Machiavelli's Philosophy." University of Toronto Press, 2019.

8. Rahe, Paul A. "Republics Ancient and Modern: Classical Republicanism and the American Revolution." University of North Carolina Press, 1992.

9. Strauss, Leo. "Thoughts on Machiavelli." University of Chicago Press, 2017.

10. Nederman, Cary J. "Machiavelli: A Beginner's Guide." Oneworld Publications, 2009.

11. de Alvarez, Leo Paul S. "Interpreting Machiavelli: Contexts, Texts, Reception." Duquesne University Press, 2013.

12. Najemy, John M. "Between Friends: Discourses of Power and Desire in the Machiavelli-Vettori Letters of 1513-1515." Princeton University Press, 1993.

13. Copenhaver, Brian P. "Machiavelli: A Portrait." The Belknap Press of Harvard University Press, 2019.

14. Bondanella, Peter, and Mark Musa. "The Portable Machiavelli." Penguin Classics, 1979.

15. Skinner, Quentin. "Machiavelli: A Beginner's Guide." Oneworld Publications, 2009.

BOOKS BY THIS AUTHOR

Philosophy And Transcendence: The Life And Works Of Giovanni Pico Della Mirandola

"Philosophy and Transcendence" is a captivating exploration of the life and works of Giovanni Pico della Mirandola, a Renaissance philosopher whose ideas challenged the traditional views of his time. This book delves deep into Pico's transformative power of knowledge and his belief in personal and spiritual growth, and how these ideas influenced his works on philosophy, theology, and mysticism. Through a comprehensive analysis of his major works such as "Oration on the Dignity of Man" and "900 Theses," the reader will be taken on a journey of intellectual discovery, exploring Pico's views on the human condition, the role of God in the universe, and the transformative power of knowledge. With its engaging prose and insightful analysis, "Philosophy and Transcendence" is a must-read for anyone interested in the Renaissance period and the evolution of philosophical thought.

Asking Good Questions: Unleashing Curiosity For Personal And Professional Growth

Step into a world where questions reign supreme, where curiosity is the driving force behind remarkable achievements. Welcome to the transformative realm of "Asking Good Questions," a captivating book that unveils the secrets to unlocking your full potential through the art of inquiry.

Embark on a captivating journey as you delve into the importance of asking good questions in every facet of your life. From the moment you crack open this compelling guide, you'll be transported into a world where clarity, relevance, and open-endedness become your guiding principles.

Immerse yourself in the sheer power of thought-provoking questions that challenge the status quo and propel you towards innovative thinking. Discover how contextual questioning can breathe life into your conversations, allowing you to navigate diverse situations with ease and finesse.

Explore the art of follow-up and active listening, honing your skills to build meaningful connections and extract deeper insights from those around you. Witness firsthand how different types of questions unlock doors to personal growth, forge stronger relationships, and drive success in business and leadership.

As you journey through the pages of "Asking Good Questions," you'll encounter invaluable tips, practical advice, and actionable strategies that enhance your questioning skills. Whether you're a student, a professional, or an aspiring leader, this book provides the roadmap to sharpening your ability to inquire, challenge, and explore.

With clarity and precision, this work tackles the common obstacles that may impede your questioning prowess. Learn how to overcome them and unleash your curiosity, tapping into a wellspring of inspiration and knowledge that will fuel your personal and professional growth.